# STRANGE ENCOUNTER AT THE SHAKESPEARE MOTEL

*poems by*

# Herb Guggenheim

*Finishing Line Press*
Georgetown, Kentucky

# STRANGE ENCOUNTER AT THE SHAKESPEARE MOTEL

Copyright © 2017 by Herbert S. Guggenheim
ISBN 978-1-62229-935-5  First Edition, Second Printing
All rights reserved under International and Pan-American Copyright Conventions. No part of this book may be reproduced in any manner whatsoever without written permission from the publisher, except in the case of brief quotations embodied in critical articles and reviews.

ACKNOWLEDGMENTS

The author wishes to acknowledge the editors of the following publications in which the accompanying poems originally appeared, some in slightly different versions.

*The Camel Saloon:* "Helmet Diving"
*Chrome Baby:* "Fall"
*District Lines:* "Post-Cold War"
*Eunoia Review:* "The Death Poem"*
*Gargoyle:* "Athena," "Date," and "Laser"
*Jellyfish Whispers:* "Wave"
*The Main Street Rag:* "Nice Ass"
*Poetry Quarterly:* "The Nicholas Brothers"
*Pyrokinection:* "Drugged"

*"The Death Poem" was also included in the author's self-published book **Sunset at the Hotel Mira Mar: New and Selected Poems.**

Publisher: Leah Maines
Editor: Christen Kincaid
Cover Art: Zaretskaya (Dreamstime.com)
Author Photo: Leslie E.Carroll
Cover Design: Elizabeth Maines McCleavy


Printed in the USA on acid-free paper.
Order online: www.finishinglinepress.com
　　　　　also available on amazon.com

Author inquiries and mail orders:
Finishing Line Press
P. O. Box 1626
Georgetown, Kentucky 40324
U. S. A.

# Table of Contents

Beverly .................................................................................. 1

Athena .................................................................................. 3

Date ...................................................................................... 6

Nice Ass ............................................................................... 8

Laser ................................................................................... 10

Post-Cold War ................................................................... 12

Caught ................................................................................ 14

Fall ...................................................................................... 16

Wave ................................................................................... 19

The Nicholas Brothers ...................................................... 21

Helmet Diving ................................................................... 24

Drugged ............................................................................. 26

The Death Poem ............................................................... 29

*This book is dedicated to Henry Taylor and Allan Lefcowitz*

**BEVERLY**

It's 2:49 AM and, on your way to the bathroom to pee, you feel a kind
        of *squish*
as you step, barefoot, into a small mound of cat vomit.

And, for some reason, you remember Beverly—
that girl you knew when you were fifteen—

how, when she got out of the back of her older brother's truck,
you thought, *Oh, my God, she's too good looking to date!*

She with her straight blonde hair and tight hip hugger jeans—
looking for all the world like those girls at the beach who spent their
        days laughing at guys like you.

For some reason, she thought you were OK
in your homemade dashiki and double knit tan slacks. And—

after four hours of anxious talk—
you got your nerve up and asked if you could kiss her.

She said *yes* and let you run your hands down the length of her
        straight blonde hair,
let you lift her tie-dyed belly shirt and cup her pale white
        breasts in your hands.

One night, her parents weren't going to be able to pick her up—they
        lived forty miles away—
so your parents said that wouldn't be a problem—that Beverly could
        bring an overnight bag and stay in the guest room.

You couldn't sleep all night
knowing she was there.

At 6:00 AM, you stole into her room and woke her up.
She said, "Hi," in a sleepy whisper

and made room for you to lie next to her in that little narrow bed.
She was wearing "shorty" pajamas.

And she let you slide your hand inside one of the leg openings—
      something you had never done before—
and you were on the cusp of a violent explosion when

prudence dictated that you lock the door.
So you staggered to your feet and started trying to quietly get it shut.

But the new carpet made it hard to close that door completely
and your father woke up.

"What's that noise?" he said from your parents' bedroom.
"What's going on out there?"

"Nothing," you said
and crept back to your room with its black light posters and model
      sailboat.

Now you're fifty-five.
It's 2:49 AM and the cat puke is cold.

## ATHENA

Your mom would leave at four to pick your dad up
and you'd have the house to yourself for about an hour.

One afternoon Athena came over to visit.
She took the bus since neither of you drove yet.

The two of you went upstairs to your bedroom.
She kicked her shoes off, you untied your Keds.

A minute later both of you were naked.
You felt like you were going to explode.

You *did it*—then jumped up and put your clothes on
but Athena lay there staring into space.

She wiped some perspiration from her forehead
and murmured that she'd love to take a shower.

Only, the shower in the hall bathroom was broken
and she said she didn't want to use the tub.
The bathroom downstairs didn't have a shower.
Your parents had the only one that worked.

You didn't really want Athena to use it
but she told you she'd feel yucky if she didn't.

So, in your parents' bathroom, you peeked out
the window to make sure they weren't coming.
Athena took her long black hair and tucked it
inside your mother's plastic shower cap.
She ran the water, stepped into the shower.

Soon your parents' Chevrolet Impala
came down the street and pulled into the driveway.

"I'll stall them at the door but you've gotta hurry."

"Hey, wait! Don't go yet! I don't have a towel."

"Use one of theirs. Just leave it on the towel rack."

You shot downstairs and flung the front door open.
"Hi!" you said, not moving from the foyer.
"Athena's here. We're upstairs doing homework."

"The Greek?" your father said, displaying brilliance.

Your mom walked past you, went into the kitchen.
Your dad went off to watch TV and smoke.
You joined your mother at the kitchen table.
"I left my sewing box upstairs," she said.

"I'll get it for you," you said nonchalantly.

"No, I'll go up. You don't know where I put it."

"I do! I do! Sit down! It's in the guest room!"

You ran upstairs just as Athena darted
naked from your parents' room to yours.

She started getting dressed. You closed the door,
grabbed the sewing box, and ran downstairs.
Athena came down carrying her school books,
acting like she'd just been doing homework.

You walked her to the bus stop. She was quiet.

At last she said, "I wish we'd had more time."

"I thought that was fantastic, didn't you?"

"Maybe next time you can come to my house."

The bus pulled up. She kissed you. You walked home.

## DATE

One night, in late May when it was warm,
you went to Bambie Larkin's house for the first and only time.

She was sexy in a fortyish "older woman" sort of way—
always smelled like perfume,

always wore dresses that were just a little bit
too short. And you wanted her—this *divorcée,* this *mom.*

But it took you by surprise when you discovered that her house was a
     mess—
and not just sort of.

The smell of cat urine hung in the motionless air,
making you wonder if she ever opened a window.

Only a sofa was clearly visible.
The rest of the furniture and whatever else she owned was gathered
     under tarps.

Cats roamed the house in search of food. Dogs barked and yelped
     from behind closed doors.
She wanted you to stay the night.

But one of the dogs was in her bedroom and she didn't feel she could
     let him out
because he was mean.

So she took you to what was sometimes her son's room
but when she opened up his fold-out couch

you both discovered that his stained mattress was covered with bread
     crumbs
(at least you hoped that's what they were).

She brushed them onto the floor and went to the closet—

brought out a brand new sheet—still in its plastic wrapper—

bit the package open
and you made frantic love on that stiff and itchy sheet.

Afterwards, you went naked into her bathroom,
felt cat litter on the tile under foot.

The bathroom reeked of Pine-Sol
like she'd tried to swab it down just before your visit.

You're no genius but you knew
you had to get the hell out of there.

So you said you had to be at work super super early the next morning
and then you escaped into the soft suburban night.

Now, twenty-six years later,
you wonder what's become of Bambie Larkin and why you never
      talked to her again.

## NICE ASS

Sometimes, when I'm in the city
walking down a crowded street on a warm spring day
looking at the women walking ahead of me—
in their jeans and shorts, their dresses, skirts, and slacks—
sometimes, I see something so stellar—so
*original*—that I want to cry out in a loud clear voice: "*Nice ass!*"—
not to bother them or anything
but simply because I want to acknowledge it—
this undeniable fact—
this Truth of Nature.

And then I think: What if I *could* say it?
and what if the woman I said it to was kind
and what if after my exclamation she said
"Oh, do you really think so? Tell me about *you*.
You seem like you must be an artist or a poet."
And I admit shyly that, yes, I've dabbled a bit in the arts
and she asks me if I'd mind going to a coffee shop because she has
aesthetic questions and thinks I might have answers.

But this is the real world and I know that I could never—
*would* never—say such a thing. But
it's sort of there all the time
on the tip of my tongue—a persistent whisper in my brain.

And then I think there are probably billions of men all over the
        world—
each with his own version of the phrase *Nice ass!*—
billions of men suppressing their impulse to say it.
And there must be billions of women—
each one with her own nice ass.
And the billions of men suppress their impulse.
And the billions of women know *exactly* what the men are
        suppressing.

And I think If each man were a star,
there'd be a galaxy—

each blazing sun suffused with the thought
*Nice ass!* And the radiant light of all those stars
would burn a Truth into the Heart of the Universe.

And the women who know what men are really thinking
would turn into stars as well—another galaxy
and the two blazing galaxies would slowly merge into a giant spiral of
    light.

*

So I ended the poem there—with that *giant spiral of light* thing—
then showed it to Lisa, a colleague whose opinion I very much respect,
and eagerly awaited her response.
She handed me back the paper.
"Well, wha'd'ya think?" I said.
She tapped her fingers on her desk for a moment, stared hard at me,
then spoke: "Nice,
Ass."

## LASER

> *How easy is a bush supposed a bear!*
> —Shakespeare

We met at a *La Madeleine* and talked for hours.
The talk was easy and intimate.
I told her about my mother
and what it was like growing up an only child.

She talked about her laser hair removal treatments
and asked me to touch her legs.
I did and they were silky smooth
and it seemed as though hair had never flourished
on their gentle terrain.

She said
she'd gotten her doctor to remove
as much hair as he possibly could,
leaving just a small amount in a vital place.
She'd gone for treatment after treatment.
Now she would never have to shave her legs—or anywhere else—
again.

We'd reached the point in the evening
where we'd either part or else make love.
And, even though this was only our first time out,
we chose the latter course.
And so it was that she came to my apartment.

We started kissing
and removing each other's clothes.
And soon we were in bed.

And then I saw it,
sculpted into a keyhole shape
or maybe a fat exclamation point—
her remaining hair,
mown like a slab of close cropped zoysia grass,

And my mind flashed to an operating room,
the temperature a chilly 58°F;
a team of nurses and technicians in aquamarine scrubs,
hairnets, face masks, and latex gloves;
and an anesthesiologist close at hand
to keep the patient calm and comfortable.

And I saw the patient
wrapped from head to toe in pure white sheets
with only a small square opening to reveal
that part of her which I cannot name.

At a given signal, all put safety goggles on.
The surgeon, wearing a plastic smock.
holds the laser gun aloft,
as a rabbi would hold the Torah unto God,
then aims it down and begins to destroy
errant hair follicles inch by inch
until only the keyhole shape is left.

And, well, all I could think about
was that laser and those follicles.
And it ruined the whole damn thing.

## POST-COLD WAR

Night.

Driving down East-West Highway, we see it—
emanating from behind us,
casting pink white light onto our dashboard, mirrors, and windshield.
It swells to a brightness we've never seen before,
bears down on us like maybe a trucker's fallen asleep—only brighter.

*Oh my God!* I think
(because I don't have original thoughts at times like this)
*It's the end!*
*Somebody just detonated something bad—*
*really bad.*

And I wonder—
as I've sometimes wondered in the past—
if it *is* something bad,
will it vaporize my brain before signals of pain, loss, and regret
       ever have a chance to reach it?
One can only hope.

Then, I wonder if it's the Christian End Time—
*The Rapture* I think they call it.
Or that gremlin Shatner sees on *The Twilight Zone*. Only
we're not on an airplane
and I'm not Shatner.

As it turns out, it's none of these things.

My wife, who's very observant,
spots sparks showering down from a fast receding phone pole
like the dying trails of some Disney World skyrocket.

A transformer's blown and,
what with all the bends in the road,
we're not sure if any other drivers got the full impact like we did.

Streetlights are out of course.
Houses are dark and we're concentrating on the road
so it doesn't occur to us to fire up our cell phones and alert the power
    company that the Rapture's starting up so they'd better send
    some men.
That call will just have to wait.

At least now, I think,
if the end does come,
I'll sort of know what to expect.

## CAUGHT

I thought I'd done everything right—
scoured the apartment for forgotten earrings
and left-behind barrettes,

sequestered the blue panties
that lay twisted up
by the side of the bed,

plucked a Kleenex
smeared with lipstick and mascara
from the trashcan,

laundered the still-damp sheets,
and remade the bed
so it looked like nothing out of the ordinary had happened.

I made it a point to leave through back entrances,
avoid familiar haunts,
and move through the shadows.

And I did my best to never speak of her or—
if I did—
to speak only in passing.

When she'd given me gifts,
I'd artfully concealed them,
carefully stashed them away.

I'd deleted her emails,
shredded her cards and letters,
and returned our wineglasses to their shelf above the sink.

But I was caught.

Apparently,
I'd failed to notice her latest opus—
the one with the subject line *x-o-x-o*.

I'd been going blithely about my business for several days
and I was feeling pretty good—
*relieved* even. Then,

one night,
my wife slammed me,
wanted to know who'd sent me that email—who the other woman
........was.

She'd been waiting days to do it,
carefully biding her time till my guard was down,
till I was about to settle in for the final episode of *Lost*.

I listened to her rant for several hours—
completely missed my program—but
she was right and there really wasn't anything I could say.

## FALL

One Sunday when you're taking out the trash
you realize it's finally gotten too cold for shorts.
So you put on jeans, a flannel shirt, and sneakers,
don your leather jacket, and go out.

Your neighborhood is old; the houses, modest.
The sidewalks and the streets are strewn with leaves.
Smoke is rising from a neighbor's chimney
and the smell of burning wood is in the air.

You head toward the park and take the trail
that parallels the creek. You walk beneath
a canopy of red and orange leaves.
Leaves have fallen all along the pathway
and you listen to them rustle underfoot.

When you get home you notice something strange—
just as you're about to pet the cats,
you see that leaves are scattered on the floor
both in the foyer and the living room.
Your wife is cooking dinner in the kitchen
and leaves are on the floor in there as well.

She doesn't make anything of it,
says she's noticed the leaves
but they don't bother her.
Beyond that she doesn't comment.

The next morning when you wake up
your bed is covered with leaves.
They're like a second blanket
and they go flying everywhere
when you throw back the covers.

Downstairs in the living room
they're at least a foot deep.
Your cats plow through them

and chase each other about
as if nothing in particular is wrong.
The entire house smells like dry leaves.

You go to work.

In the evening
you open your front door
and a cascade of leaves
spills out onto the porch
You wade through them
and find your wife
half buried,
busily answering emails on her laptop.
The cats are asleep on the bookshelf—
the only piece of furniture you can see.

Later,
you and your wife clear off the bed
as best you can
and settle in for the night.
But you feel uneasy
and find it hard to rest.

In the morning, you go to work.

When you return home
at dusk,
you see that the house itself
has *become*
a house of leaves.

Your wife is standing outside,
wearing her winter coat,
holding the cat carrier in one hand
and her computer in the other.

"We can't live in it now," she says.
"The whole place is made of leaves."

Just then you feel a blast of cold wind
and you watch as your house collapses and scatters.

"We'll have to go to a shelter," you say.

## WAVE

In Bermuda—
at Elbow Beach—
the ocean is swimming pool blue—
so clear that you can still see your toes
when you've waded out as far as you can go.

The waves at Elbow Beach are gentle mostly
but occasionally a giant one rolls in
almost in slow motion—
almost like liquid glass.

If you have your back to it,
you might not realize it's coming till the last second
and the wave washes over your head
and you're spitting out salt water
which you didn't mean to drink.

When my wife and I get out of the ocean,
a wave follows us back to our cruise ship.

We return home
and the wave is right behind us.
It accompanies me to my office
and comes home with me at night.

Sometimes the wave sleeps by the fireplace.
At other times I open the bedroom closet
and the wave jumps out,
surprising both me and my wife.

When we're out and about,
the wave spots some innocent bystanders
and washes over them,
leaving them speechless, spluttering, and a bit confused.
Also wet.

Eventually the wave gets homesick

and books a flight to Bermuda.
It flies coach,
gets a middle seat
and feels uncomfortable the whole way back.

When the plane lands,
the wave boards a bus
and rides back to Elbow Beach
where it crosses the sand and slides back into the ocean.

We never hear from the wave again.

*for Leslie Elizabeth Carroll*

## THE NICHOLAS BROTHERS

It's dusk and it's about to rain.
My wife's volunteering at the hospice,
which means it's my night to order pizza
which isn't good for me
but what the hell.

The wind is whipping up
and I'm lucky to make it to my porch before the sky splits open.

Leaning against the front door is a package.
I bring it in, glad it didn't get wet.

It's the movie *Stormy Weather* on DVD.
Who sent it? I wonder.
No note.
I don't have a clue.

When the Domino's man brings my pizza,
I put the movie on and settle in.

The story unfolds and eventually
we find ourselves at a nightclub on the evening of the Big Show.
Cab Calloway is singing "Jumpin' Jive."
His band is *smokin'* and he owns the room.

Baton in hand,
he strides over to a table and he scats.
The two gents at the table scat back.
Then they start to seriously tap.

The gents jump onto flat topped music stands, flying
from one to the next to the next.
They execute a series of impossible moves
then dance over to a giant double staircase.
Each step is two feet high but they don't care.
They run-dance to the platform at the top.
To get back down they leapfrog stair to stair,

each jump they take ending in a split.

I put my slice of pizza down and stop the movie.
I can't watch any more.
They're too good.

Just then there's a knock at my front door.
I open it and—
it's them
in tie and tails,
holding umbrellas,
looking like they just stepped out of 1943.
"May we come in?" they ask.
"Uh, sure," I say.

"Nice time vortex you have out there,"
Fayard the older brother comments.
"I'm not aware of any—" I start
but Harold, the younger one, pats me on the back:
"We're gonna teach you how to tap."

They show me a thousand steps
but I can't do any of them.

"Come with us," they say, grabbing their umbrellas.
They throw open the big double window,
jump out, and just sort of float
about thirty feet off the ground,
waiting for me to follow.

I stand there like a doofus.
I'm afraid to jump.
"I can't," I say.

"Don't worry. We'll be back," Harold shouts.
"But right now we've got to
save the world from great and terrible evil."

So I watch,
knowing I'll never be that good at anything,
as they go flying
off into the stormy night.

## HELMET DIVING

You stand at the edge of a floating wooden platform
and step onto the first rung of a ladder
that plunges straight down into the ocean.

They've told you it's easy—
that even an eight-year-old can do it.
But you're strangely unconvinced.
After all, stuff happens. Bad stuff.

The helmet they place over your head weighs seventy-five pounds
but you won't feel it, they've told you,
once you get below the surface.

You listen to the echo of your breathing
and realize that the air flowing in through a thin yellow tube
is probably the only thing between you and death.

When you reach the sea floor,
you're down a mere twenty feet.
Still, that's not bad for someone like you
who doesn't know his ass from a hole in the ground.

The water is clear and blue at once.
Schools of fish swim by—
tiger fish with black and orange stripes,
pale translucent fish, fish of blue and silver.

You spend the next thirty minutes on a trail
that takes you past sunken helicopters, rock formations,
sea anemones, and living coral,

Scuba divers watch you,
making sure you and the others are safe.
One diver holds up a sea urchin,
places it in your palm,
then returns it to the ocean floor.
Another hands you a fistful of ground up *something*.

At the smell of it, a cloud of fish envelops you,
eating from your open hand,
their tiny teeth scraping your palm.
In seconds, the food is gone.

Eventually, the scuba divers signal
that it's time to return to the surface.
You ascend the ladder.

At the top, someone lifts the helmet off your head.
You've made it.
The adventure has come to an end.
Everything else you're afraid of lies ahead.

## DRUGGED

The last time you took Ambien,
you were on vacation in Vancouver, British Columbia,
staying at a small respectable hotel.

Your wife was asleep and you were asleep
but, at a certain moment,
you got up—

perhaps to use the bathroom,
perhaps driven by some other imperative in your dream—
and the story gets murky after that.

You must have gone through a doorway—
and the door must have locked behind you—
and you must have felt that you couldn't get back in.

So you went forward—
down a long hall
then through a second doorway,

down a flight of stairs
then through another door
that also locked.

You're not sure what happened after that
but, when your feet hit the cold pavement
and you felt the cool spring breeze against your ass,

you woke up enough to know
that you were standing outside
*in a foreign country*

wearing nothing but a t-shirt
and that a busy 24-hour McDonald's
was just two doors away.

Peering in through the hotel's glass door,

you could see that most of the lobby lights were off—
the front desk, dark.

Without the benefit of glasses,
you squinted at the instructions on the hotel entry system
then punched in the designated code.

A man picked up.
"I was sleep walking," you carefully explained.
"And I'm standing here not wearing any pants."

After a thoughtful silence, he asked for your room number,
your name, your wife's name then said,
"I'll be down."

Eventually,
he came and let you in,
walked you to the elevator,

put in his card key,
pressed the button for your floor
then jumped back out as if you were a monster.

You ascended to your floor
where your sleepy wife met you,
wrapped you in a blanket,

and brought you back to your hotel room
where you immediately fell back into bed.
In the morning, at first, you thought you'd dreamt it

but when you asked your wife,
she told you that you hadn't.
Now, reflecting on it,

you realize that life propels us forward
and that all the doors behind us click shut.

We can't go back.

In a way, you think,
we're always standing naked at the door—
our bodies roused by an insistent breeze.

## THE DEATH POEM

Congratulations!
You've drawn the Death Card—
the Ace of Spades.

1.

In the morning, before work, you lie in the bathtub
and lather your body with oatmeal and honey soap.
The bathwater becomes cloudy and,
as you eye the expanse of your body partially submerged beneath it,
you imagine that the bathtub is no longer a bath
but a long satin-lined coffin
and that you are a corpse
lying in state.

2.

It can happen at any time—
this death.

You are a child in a nursery school,
playing with giant multi-colored blocks.
You've just had your morning glass of juice—
and cookies—vanilla wafers probably.
A fragrant spring breeze drifts in through an opened window.

But, unbeknownst to you,
a terrorist has planted a bomb.
It explodes
and you, most of your classmates, and your teacher
all die.

One child lives
but she is badly maimed and will not lead a normal life.

3.

This consciousness that you treasure and struggle to enrich—
this consciousness—
that takes courses,
reads books,
and sometimes learns from past errors—

this consciousness
that you have right now—
will grow dim at first,
perhaps or perhaps not,
and will stop being consciousness.
Everything—
all your experiences,
all your hopes and dreams and insights—
will be as if they never were.

In fact,
there will be no *you*
anymore.

4.

You take pills at night.
You know that if you take too many pills you will die.

The choice is yours.

5.

You are driving,
trying to remember which road you take,
which exit you get off at.
Cars stream by around you and make no sense.
You are lost.

When you finally do arrive home,
you try to remember what you went out for.

You want to play a CD
but you can't remember the name of that Italian singer—
the one who sang that song about—
about San Francisco.

Hours later, your doorbell rings.
You answer it.
A woman is standing there.
She says, "*Jeez*, I was worried sick about you."
And you look at her and try to remember her name.
She seems so familiar.
And maybe she's your daughter.
Yes, she certainly must be.

"Dad—?" she says.

6.

You are in a darkened bedroom
making love to someone you hardly know.
You are hovering at the edge of an orgasm.
You reach it and make a loud noise.
You clench your partner hard for a time
then gradually relax.
The orgasm was wonderful, you think to yourself.
Then you roll over onto your designated side of the bed and think:
*No matter how many times I do this, there will always be death.*

7.

A scoutmaster enters a woman's home.
She doesn't know him.
The woman's ten-year-old daughter is doing an art project on the
    kitchen table.

He tells her that he wants to talk to her mother privately and asks her to wait for him to finish.
He takes the mother into her bedroom and tells her he's going to kill her by putting a plastic bag over her head and strangling her until he feels her die.

8.

A 56-year-old man sits on a bench at the park, reading a book.
He takes blood pressure medication but it's not working today.
At dusk, a park policeman, riding on horseback,
finds him on the ground in front of the bench—dead.
The man was never married and neither is the park policeman.

9.

Lillian feels isolated and alone.
Her boyfriend of three months has left her,
telling her he just can't put up with her shit.
Lillian is 43.

She cooks dinner for a close male friend and his 10-year-old daughter.
After dinner, she gives the child a present—
a box containing some of her favorite keepsakes.

When they're gone, she does the dishes and takes a jar of pills from the kitchen cabinet.
She's been saving them for just this occasion.
She undresses, puts on a nightgown, pours herself a glass of chardonnay, and takes the pills.
She gets into bed, swallows some more pills, and waits.

Herb Guggenheim was born in Washington, D.C. and raised in Silver Spring, Maryland. After barely graduating from high school and stumbling through four years of college, Herb crash-landed in graduate school, studying creative writing at American University, the University of Southern Mississippi, and Johns Hopkins University. He studied poetry writing with Pulitzer Prize winner Henry Taylor, fiction writing with award-winning novelists Frederick Barthelme and John Barth.

After earning an MA from the Writing Seminars at Johns Hopkins, Herb taught English and creative writing at several colleges and universities. Finding himself suddenly middle-aged and, craving a change of pace, he became a licensed clinical social worker and currently maintains a small private practice in the D.C. suburbs.

Over the years, Herb's poems and short stories have appeared in a number of magazines, including the *Beloit Poetry Journal, Chrome Baby,* the *Eunoia Review,* the *Florida Review, Gargoyle, Gutter Eloquence, Kalkion,* the *Main Street Rag, Poetry Quarterly, Schlock,* the *Unrorean,* and the *Washington Review.*

Herb's poetry has been nominated for a Pushcart Prize, a Best of the Net award, and has received four honorable mentions in the *Writer's Digest* annual writing competition. At this writing, his novel *Violations of Causality* is a finalist in the Foreword INDIES 2016 Book of the Year Award competition.

www.ingramcontent.com/pod-product-compliance
Lightning Source LLC
LaVergne TN
LVHW041604070426
835507LV00011B/1294